# An
# ADVENTUROUS
# LIFE

Your diary of fulfillment,
self-expression, and spontaneity

**LifeAdventure**

THE JOY OF ADVENTURE IS AN ANTICIPATION
OF THE JOY OF SUCCESS

ONCE THE PROBLEM HAS BEEN RAISED
IT MUST BE RESOLVED AND THE
ADVENTURE HAS BEGUN

ADVENTURE CEASES AS SOON
AS NORMALCY BEGINS*

_____
* Quotes from Paul Tournier

Do you feel like you are missing out on life? Is life passing you by? **Does it look like others are actually going somewhere while you are stuck in a hopeless monotony, following some unwritten rule that has an overwhelming, inhibiting power over your life?** Do you crave exaltation, excitement, rejuvenation or renewal?

In fact, most of us do. We are hungry for **the miraculous power of novelty and enterprise because it makes us feel alive**. Living on autopilot performing daily tasks is not life, no matter how much gratitude or positive thinking you pour into it. We are meant to be inventors and creators, in the image of god; the greatest creator of all. When we try to figure things out and imagine solutions to our dilemmas and challenges, the adventure begins. **The exhilaration of taking a risk and setting off on a new path is the most underestimated human need there is**.

Thanks to this diary, you will find and target the adventures worth chasing, **UNIQUE TO YOU**. By pondering on basic questions we provide, focusing on your adventurous, spontaneous self will become second nature. Start living!

# DEAR READER,

If you picked up this diary, most likely you are looking for a kind of **a mad-scientist, excited-kid uplifting emotion** in your life. It sounds attractive because we instinctively believe that life can be adventurous, exciting, and fulfilling, and because there are other people who live like that. We love reading and watching movies about their amazing lives, full of twists and turns, ups and downs, mentally identifying with them, and sometimes envying their luck and achievements.

**How can we become like them?** Their inventions and discoveries are amazing but seem completely out of reach. Actually, we don't even want such high levels of achievement. **It's the process; the burning passion they had throughout their lives** that seems so much more desirable than the routine we are stuck with.

There was a time, though, when they too were like us, the hopeless nonentities we consider ourselves to be. Usually, their story goes that yes, they were nobodies, but they had a dream, a dilemma, a question, and an urge to solve it. They took it seriously, even though other smart, successful people around them did not.

You often hear phrases like, "I did it because I believed in myself." "You gotta believe in yourself," is probably one the most annoying phrases you can hear if you are someone who is stuck and doesn't even know where to start looking. If I am not some kind of an athlete training for the Olympics, I go to work, come home, do what I am supposed to do, what can I possibly "believe in." That I can pay my bills?

Perhaps, we can believe for a moment **that what we love is lovable**, and **our questions and doubts are interesting and valid**, even if only for us for the time being. In fact,

**this could be the main difference between us, ordinary mortals, and them, the lucky chosen ones**. They give their thoughts weight and look for answers, while we regard ours as silly and undeserving; we don't even pay attention to them.

Maybe this is the reason that it's easier for children to follow the footsteps of their creative parents. It's not just talent. **If you grow up learning about creative people's habits, you know about the creative process and it's easier to repeat it using your own thoughts**. Some of it could be as simple as keeping a small notepad handy to write your ideas down. Children coming from a creative background have it because their father/mother did but you don't, and you have forgotten all about your ideas or musings.

To sum up, these amazing people had a plan that was born out of a desire to figure things out; a question that had not been asked or answered **in a manner that was right for them**. Creativity and invention came as a consequence of their trying to find something out, an act of problem-solving. There was also an element of risk involved, meaning that the outcome was never known. This, too, made their endeavors exciting. It was not necessarily the end result, but rather the process where they applied themselves fully while pursuing success.

If we were to come up with **an exciting life formula**, it would look something like this:

**An exciting life is creative problem-solving for a person's distinct dilemmas, risk-taking, and expectation of success.**

Of course, not all of us will turn into Newtons or Einsteins because we creatively solve our dilemmas but **we can, and we must, fulfill ourselves**.

This diary will be **your aide in learning how to give importance to your dilemmas/longings/doubts/**

**predicaments, and how to find your path to invention, creativity, and, ultimately, a fruitful life.**

How does one go about finding big, exciting projects? To begin with, it is important that we **focus on all of our dilemmas and issues every day, even minor ones** (first question in the diary), such as should I buy a new table or keep the old one or do I go out or make food at home, etc. **They are our training ground for catching our unique spontaneous solution vibe**. Here is how it works.

Perhaps you had a moment like this in your life: your something breaks (car?) and you feel desperate because you really need it and don't know what to do. All of a sudden, out of nowhere, the name of a person who can help you pops up in your mind (a friend's friend or something like that). Maybe an hour beforehand, you wouldn't have thought of that person even if you had wanted to but, surprisingly, you did now. **Eureka!**

**All ideas, big and small, come this way.** We scratch our heads, search, read, think, but when we are looking for a solution, we don't need to fret, and worry, because it comes on its own, suddenly, and unexpectedly. Obviously, some tasks need to be attended to in a timely fashion — kids need to be fed, washed, and taken care of, and food has to be bought and cooked. But when some procrastinating is tolerable, like maybe when deciding whether to clean the car today or in a week, **a decision can be reached in a satisfactory, comfortable, sort-of-cosmic, non-coercive way.** Wait until you feel like doing whatever you need to do, or wait for ideas to appear on how to motivate yourself.

Something along these lines could work: I really don't feel like doing it — I will ask so-and-so — no, they won't do a good job. Maybe I will put some music on and just do it — I will think about it later. OK, I got it. I'll do it when I have very little time so it's just done quickly.

It may sound silly — just go ahead and get it done; why wait to do something so trivial even if you don't want to? But we aren't robots receiving and executing commands, and we should not treat ourselves as such. **We didn't come to this earth to perform endless tasks.**

When you reach a comfortable decision, you learn what it feels like to be sure of what you are doing. You learn that you can afford to take your time and that it is fulfilling to do things this way, even if they are simple, everyday duties. Life seems less hostile and grueling, it collaborates. This feeling is your basis for finding more solutions that are right for you, and you only.

The amount of **self-assurance, self-respect**, and **warmth towards yourself** that you feel when you reach a decision this way, no matter how minor the problem is, **will skyrocket**. Without this self-assurance, how can you believe in a project that is your own? How can you set on a new path and feel excited about it? You can't because you will be overrun by doubt and any idea that comes to you will seem worthless. Plus, you will lack the unwavering conviction you need to start acting on a decision.

You might think that you will never get anything done this way and you just wait and wait all your life. Most of the time, we do have deadlines. If you can't decide whether to go to a concert, tickets may be gone by the time you do. But then, you just know that at the moment when you were ready, the circumstances were different. It does not mean, however, that you have to betray and coerce yourself. Next time, you might decide to buy tickets earlier even if you are not sure and may consider not going and losing your money, or maybe you won't even consider any of these options. All these decisions are right: they are yours, **as long as you feel comfortable when making them.** You are searching for **tailor-made solutions** that fit you because you are worth it, and because no one else can find them for you.

In the case where you don't have a deadline, say, you want to write a book sometime in the future, your lack of fulfillment will bother you and make you decide to try something to resolve it.

Tougher dilemmas may require multi-step solutions. It's important to **pay attention to anything new, even really tiny events** that happen and give you a different outlook on your struggles, or further your understanding of them (questions in the diary). Examples could be a tiny voice in your head, a chance encounter, inspiring music on the radio, a book that catches your eye, a moment you like in a movie or a show. All those things could be useful steps towards feeling different, inspired, and trying something new. We all like a nice story about miraculous, clear-cut signs of destiny that lead us exactly where we need to go, but perhaps things in real life are a little more complex and subtle.

If, for example, you realise that you want to write a book, quite spontaneously, you start paying attention to other people's writing and how they go about doing it. You pay attention to topics they picked when you happen to hear their podcast, you read books about creativity and writing and suddenly, the image of how it's done becomes sharper and sharper in your mind. **The source of your motivation** for taking all these steps is not coercion, fear, or anxiety but **interest in your own curiosity, your interests, and ideas.** Write them all down in the diary, don't discard anything as unworthy. If they just came to you, they are both yours and not, so maybe treasuring them as gifts would be a good idea.

To recap, most of the time, just being aware of your dilemmas is enough to have **solutions start flowing naturally**. We kind of know it already but a mere understanding of this process liberates us from the unnecessary pressure and anxiety we tend to feel when looking for an answer. When no solution is immediately clear and satisfactory, keep looking, search and wait, maybe resort to your pop-up solution places — the shower, a car ride, a train ride, a cup of coffee, favorite music, a walk, vacuuming — whatever works for you (note and make a list of those in the diary). **A solution will come, it will be exciting, and it will feel right.**

Remember that all discoveries were made this way. Mendeleyev searched and studied for years but his periodic table appeared to him in a dream. It works for ordinary folk too: you don't have to be a genius scientist looking for a scientific breakthrough.

Try it and you will soon realize that you are not alone struggling to navigate the ups and downs of life but **everything in the universe, even your shower, cup of coffee, and walk, is participating and giving you a hand.**

With that in mind, embark on **your most coveted adventures!**

## IN A NUTSHELL:

List 10 things that really bother you in your life.

Turn attention to your emotions, impulses, and dilemmas throughout the day.

Watch for feedback: solutions, suggestions, insights, and thoughts will pop up in your mind.

Track everything down at the end of the day in the diary or, if you are tight on time, answer the questions in your mind.

Start over the next day; tomorrow is a new day.

Re-evaluate your overall outlook after 21 days of diary writing.

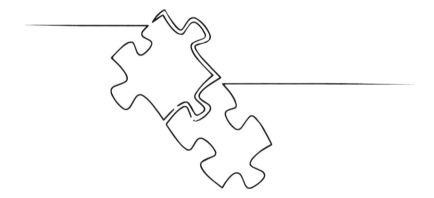

List up to 10 main struggles/worries/longings/challenges/ problems that, if solved, would definitely make your life easier and better. Think and dream big. Be silly if you wish.

_____

_____

_____

_____

_____

_____

_____

_____

_____

_____

_____

_____

_____

Number them in the order of importance.

Select top 3 problems that are always on your mind and write them down

1 _____

2 _____

3 _____

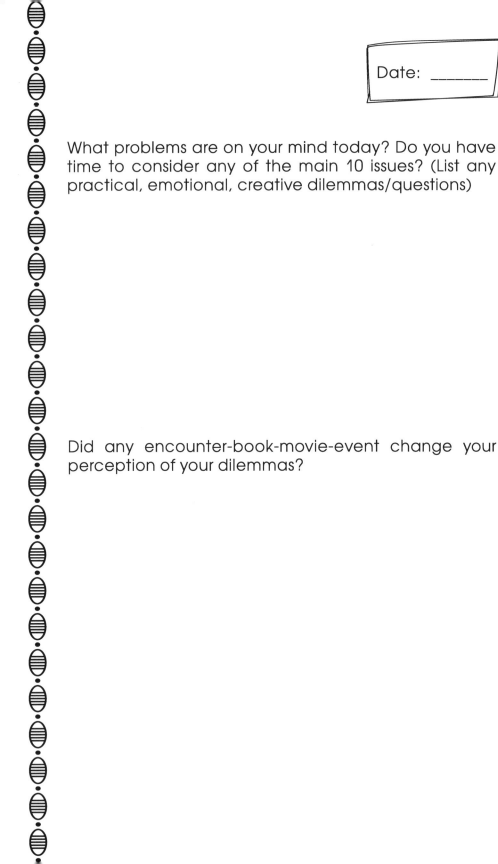

Date: _____

What problems are on your mind today? Do you have time to consider any of the main 10 issues? (List any practical, emotional, creative dilemmas/questions)

Did any encounter-book-movie-event change your perception of your dilemmas?

Did any solutions pop up in your mind? Where were you when it happened? What were you doing at the time?

Does anything feel new?

What problems are on your mind today? Do you have time to consider any of the main 10 issues? (List any practical, emotional, creative dilemmas/questions)

Did any encounter-book-movie-event change your perception of your dilemmas?

Did any solutions pop up in your mind? Where were you when it happened? What were you doing at the time?

Does anything feel new?

What problems are on your mind today? Do you have time to consider any of the main 10 issues? (List any practical, emotional, creative dilemmas/questions)

Did any encounter-book-movie-event change your perception of your dilemmas?

Did any solutions pop up in your mind? Where were you when it happened? What were you doing at the time?

Does anything feel new?

What problems are on your mind today? Do you have time to consider any of the main 10 issues? (List any practical, emotional, creative dilemmas/questions)

Did any encounter-book-movie-event change your perception of your dilemmas?

Did any solutions pop up in your mind? Where were you when it happened? What were you doing at the time?

Does anything feel new?

Date: _____

What problems are on your mind today? Do you have time to consider any of the main 10 issues? (List any practical, emotional, creative dilemmas/questions)

Did any encounter-book-movie-event change your perception of your dilemmas?

Did any solutions pop up in your mind? Where were you when it happened? What were you doing at the time?

Does anything feel new?

Date: _____

What problems are on your mind today? Do you have time to consider any of the main 10 issues? (List any practical, emotional, creative dilemmas/questions)

Did any encounter-book-movie-event change your perception of your dilemmas?

Did any solutions pop up in your mind? Where were you when it happened? What were you doing at the time?

Does anything feel new?

Date: _____

What problems are on your mind today? Do you have time to consider any of the main 10 issues? (List any practical, emotional, creative dilemmas/questions)

Did any encounter-book-movie-event change your perception of your dilemmas?

Did any solutions pop up in your mind? Where were you when it happened? What were you doing at the time?

Does anything feel new?

*The instinct of adventure may be cloaked, smothered, and repressed, but it never disappears from human personality. The timidest pen-pushing clerk will disclose under psychoanalysis, and particularly in the analysis of his dreams, a secret nostalgia for the adventure which he has sacrificed to security. Without really understanding why, he will have a predilection for the most frightening of adventure films, mentally identifying himself with the hero so as to procure vicariously the joys he deprives himself in real life.»*

Paul Tournier

List movie/ book/real-life characters you have identified yourself with. What is it about them that appealed to you?

# JUST FOR FUN

Date: _____

What problems are on your mind today? Do you have time to consider any of the main 10 issues? (List any practical, emotional, creative dilemmas/questions)

Did any encounter-book-movie-event change your perception of your dilemmas?

Did any solutions pop up in your mind? Where were you when it happened? What were you doing at the time?

Does anything feel new?

What problems are on your mind today? Do you have time to consider any of the main 10 issues? (List any practical, emotional, creative dilemmas/questions)

Did any encounter-book-movie-event change your perception of your dilemmas?

Did any solutions pop up in your mind? Where were you when it happened? What were you doing at the time?

Does anything feel new?

What problems are on your mind today? Do you have time to consider any of the main 10 issues? (List any practical, emotional, creative dilemmas/questions)

Did any encounter-book-movie-event change your perception of your dilemmas?

Did any solutions pop up in your mind? Where were you when it happened? What were you doing at the time?

Does anything feel new?

What problems are on your mind today? Do you have time to consider any of the main 10 issues? (List any practical, emotional, creative dilemmas/questions)

Did any encounter-book-movie-event change your perception of your dilemmas?

Did any solutions pop up in your mind? Where were you when it happened? What were you doing at the time?

Does anything feel new?

What problems are on your mind today? Do you have time to consider any of the main 10 issues? (List any practical, emotional, creative dilemmas/questions)

Did any encounter-book-movie-event change your perception of your dilemmas?

Did any solutions pop up in your mind? Where were you when it happened? What were you doing at the time?

Does anything feel new?

What problems are on your mind today? Do you have time to consider any of the main 10 issues? (List any practical, emotional, creative dilemmas/questions)

Did any encounter-book-movie-event change your perception of your dilemmas?

Did any solutions pop up in your mind? Where were you when it happened? What were you doing at the time?

Does anything feel new?

Date: _____

What problems are on your mind today? Do you have time to consider any of the main 10 issues? (List any practical, emotional, creative dilemmas/questions)

Did any encounter-book-movie-event change your perception of your dilemmas?

Did any solutions pop up in your mind? Where were you when it happened? What were you doing at the time?

Does anything feel new?

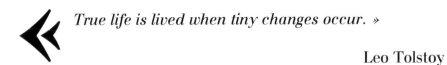

*True life is lived when tiny changes occur.* »

Leo Tolstoy

Have you noticed any tiny changes in your life since you have been working on this diary?

# JUST FOR FUN

What problems are on your mind today? Do you have time to consider any of the main 10 issues? (List any practical, emotional, creative dilemmas/questions)

Did any encounter-book-movie-event change your perception of your dilemmas?

Did any solutions pop up in your mind? Where were you when it happened? What were you doing at the time?

Does anything feel new?

What problems are on your mind today? Do you have time to consider any of the main 10 issues? (List any practical, emotional, creative dilemmas/questions)

Did any encounter-book-movie-event change your perception of your dilemmas?

Did any solutions pop up in your mind? Where were you when it happened? What were you doing at the time?

Does anything feel new?

Date: _____

What problems are on your mind today? Do you have time to consider any of the main 10 issues? (List any practical, emotional, creative dilemmas/questions)

Did any encounter-book-movie-event change your perception of your dilemmas?

Did any solutions pop up in your mind? Where were you when it happened? What were you doing at the time?

Does anything feel new?

What problems are on your mind today? Do you have time to consider any of the main 10 issues? (List any practical, emotional, creative dilemmas/questions)

Did any encounter-book-movie-event change your perception of your dilemmas?

Did any solutions pop up in your mind? Where were you when it happened? What were you doing at the time?

Does anything feel new?

What problems are on your mind today? Do you have time to consider any of the main 10 issues? (List any practical, emotional, creative dilemmas/questions)

Did any encounter-book-movie-event change your perception of your dilemmas?

Did any solutions pop up in your mind? Where were you when it happened? What were you doing at the time?

Does anything feel new?

What problems are on your mind today? Do you have time to consider any of the main 10 issues? (List any practical, emotional, creative dilemmas/questions)

Did any encounter-book-movie-event change your perception of your dilemmas?

Did any solutions pop up in your mind? Where were you when it happened? What were you doing at the time?

Does anything feel new?

What problems are on your mind today? Do you have time to consider any of the main 10 issues? (List any practical, emotional, creative dilemmas/questions)

Did any encounter-book-movie-event change your perception of your dilemmas?

Did any solutions pop up in your mind? Where were you when it happened? What were you doing at the time?

Does anything feel new?

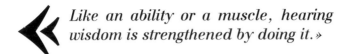 *Like an ability or a muscle, hearing   your inner wisdom is strengthened by doing it.»*

Robbie Gass

Has it become easier for you to listen to your inner wisdom since you have been working on this diary? If so, how?

Make a list of all times - circumstances- places conducive to pop-up solutions

What is the most amazing thing you discovered while working on this diary?

# Re-evaluation

List up to 10 main problems/issues/struggles/worries on your mind now and compare them to your previous list 21 days ago.

Has anything changed?

If some problems went away what is life like without them?

What will be your next life adventure?

Notes

What problems are on your mind today? Do you have time to consider any of the main 10 issues? (List any practical, emotional, creative dilemmas/questions)

Did any encounter-book-movie-event change your perception of your dilemmas?

Did any solutions pop up in your mind? Where were you when it happened? What were you doing at the time?

Does anything feel new?

What problems are on your mind today? Do you have time to consider any of the main 10 issues? (List any practical, emotional, creative dilemmas/questions)

Did any encounter-book-movie-event change your perception of your dilemmas?

Did any solutions pop up in your mind? Where were you when it happened? What were you doing at the time?

Does anything feel new?

What problems are on your mind today? Do you have time to consider any of the main 10 issues? (List any practical, emotional, creative dilemmas/questions)

Did any encounter-book-movie-event change your perception of your dilemmas?

Did any solutions pop up in your mind? Where were you when it happened? What were you doing at the time?

Does anything feel new?

What problems are on your mind today? Do you have time to consider any of the main 10 issues? (List any practical, emotional, creative dilemmas/questions)

Did any encounter-book-movie-event change your perception of your dilemmas?

Did any solutions pop up in your mind? Where were you when it happened? What were you doing at the time?

Does anything feel new?

Date: _____

What problems are on your mind today? Do you have time to consider any of the main 10 issues? (List any practical, emotional, creative dilemmas/questions)

Did any encounter-book-movie-event change your perception of your dilemmas?

Did any solutions pop up in your mind? Where were you when it happened? What were you doing at the time?

Does anything feel new?

Date: _____

What problems are on your mind today? Do you have time to consider any of the main 10 issues? (List any practical, emotional, creative dilemmas/questions)

Did any encounter-book-movie-event change your perception of your dilemmas?

Did any solutions pop up in your mind? Where were you when it happened? What were you doing at the time?

Does anything feel new?

What problems are on your mind today? Do you have time to consider any of the main 10 issues? (List any practical, emotional, creative dilemmas/questions)

Did any encounter-book-movie-event change your perception of your dilemmas?

Did any solutions pop up in your mind? Where were you when it happened? What were you doing at the time?

Does anything feel new?

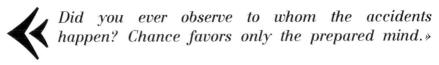 *Did you ever observe to whom the accidents happen? Chance favors only the prepared mind.»*

Louis Pasteur

Have any "accidents" happened since you have started working on this diary?

# JUST FOR FUN

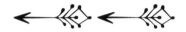

What problems are on your mind today? Do you have time to consider any of the main 10 issues? (List any practical, emotional, creative dilemmas/questions)

Did any encounter-book-movie-event change your perception of your dilemmas?

Did any solutions pop up in your mind? Where were you when it happened? What were you doing at the time?

Does anything feel new?

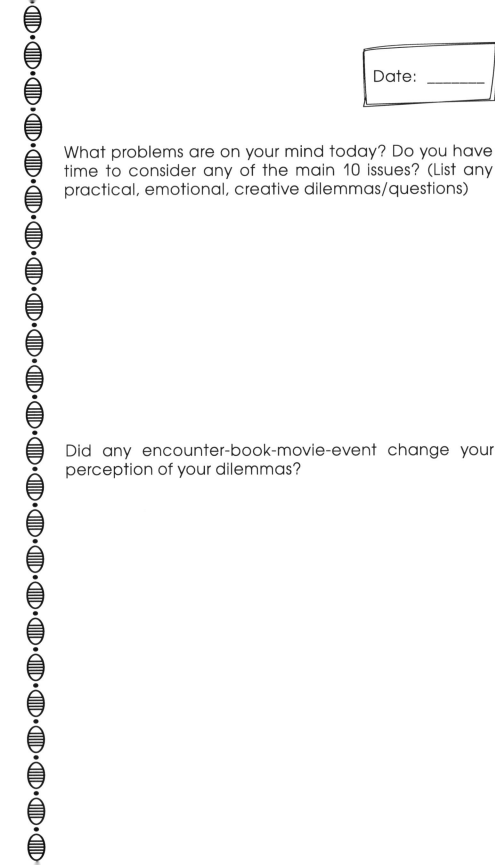

Date: _____

What problems are on your mind today? Do you have time to consider any of the main 10 issues? (List any practical, emotional, creative dilemmas/questions)

Did any encounter-book-movie-event change your perception of your dilemmas?

Did any solutions pop up in your mind? Where were you when it happened? What were you doing at the time?

Does anything feel new?

What problems are on your mind today? Do you have time to consider any of the main 10 issues? (List any practical, emotional, creative dilemmas/questions)

Did any encounter-book-movie-event change your perception of your dilemmas?

Did any solutions pop up in your mind? Where were you when it happened? What were you doing at the time?

Does anything feel new?

What problems are on your mind today? Do you have time to consider any of the main 10 issues? (List any practical, emotional, creative dilemmas/questions)

Did any encounter-book-movie-event change your perception of your dilemmas?

Did any solutions pop up in your mind? Where were you when it happened? What were you doing at the time?

Does anything feel new?

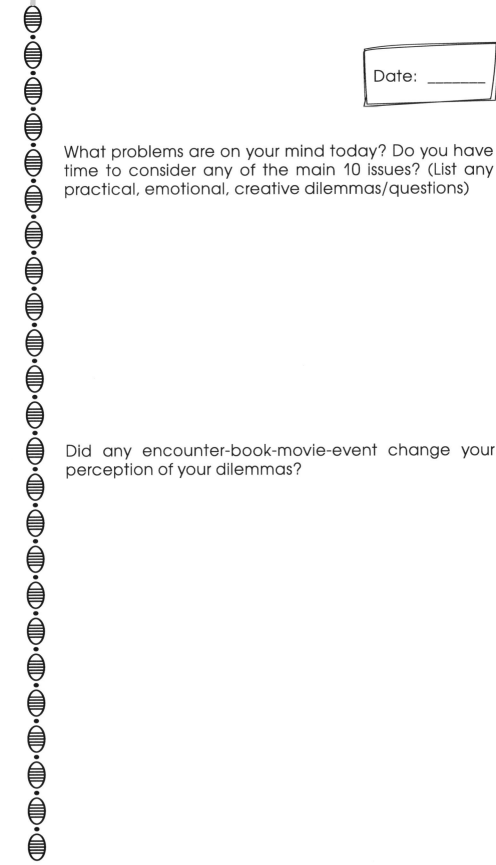

Date: _____

What problems are on your mind today? Do you have time to consider any of the main 10 issues? (List any practical, emotional, creative dilemmas/questions)

Did any encounter-book-movie-event change your perception of your dilemmas?

Did any solutions pop up in your mind? Where were you when it happened? What were you doing at the time?

Does anything feel new?

Date: _____

What problems are on your mind today? Do you have time to consider any of the main 10 issues? (List any practical, emotional, creative dilemmas/questions)

Did any encounter-book-movie-event change your perception of your dilemmas?

Did any solutions pop up in your mind? Where were you when it happened? What were you doing at the time?

Does anything feel new?

What problems are on your mind today? Do you have time to consider any of the main 10 issues? (List any practical, emotional, creative dilemmas/questions)

Did any encounter-book-movie-event change your perception of your dilemmas?

Did any solutions pop up in your mind? Where were you when it happened? What were you doing at the time?

Does anything feel new?

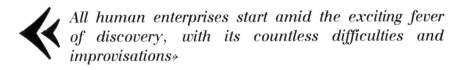 *All human enterprises start amid the exciting fever of discovery, with its countless difficulties and improvisations»*

Paul Tournier

List circumstances in your life when you felt the exciting fever of discovery.

# JUST FOR FUN

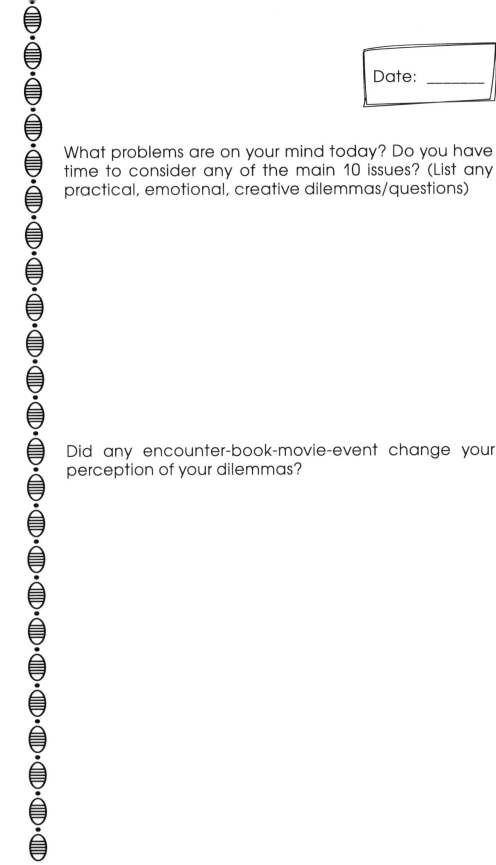

Date: _____

What problems are on your mind today? Do you have time to consider any of the main 10 issues? (List any practical, emotional, creative dilemmas/questions)

Did any encounter-book-movie-event change your perception of your dilemmas?

Did any solutions pop up in your mind? Where were you when it happened? What were you doing at the time?

Does anything feel new?

Date: _____

What problems are on your mind today? Do you have time to consider any of the main 10 issues? (List any practical, emotional, creative dilemmas/questions)

Did any encounter-book-movie-event change your perception of your dilemmas?

Did any solutions pop up in your mind? Where were you when it happened? What were you doing at the time?

Does anything feel new?

Date: _____

What problems are on your mind today? Do you have time to consider any of the main 10 issues? (List any practical, emotional, creative dilemmas/questions)

Did any encounter-book-movie-event change your perception of your dilemmas?

Did any solutions pop up in your mind? Where were you when it happened? What were you doing at the time?

Does anything feel new?

Date: _____

What problems are on your mind today? Do you have time to consider any of the main 10 issues? (List any practical, emotional, creative dilemmas/questions)

Did any encounter-book-movie-event change your perception of your dilemmas?

Did any solutions pop up in your mind? Where were you when it happened? What were you doing at the time?

Does anything feel new?

What problems are on your mind today? Do you have time to consider any of the main 10 issues? (List any practical, emotional, creative dilemmas/questions)

Did any encounter-book-movie-event change your perception of your dilemmas?

Did any solutions pop up in your mind? Where were you when it happened? What were you doing at the time?

Does anything feel new?

What problems are on your mind today? Do you have time to consider any of the main 10 issues? (List any practical, emotional, creative dilemmas/questions)

Did any encounter-book-movie-event change your perception of your dilemmas?

Did any solutions pop up in your mind? Where were you when it happened? What were you doing at the time?

Does anything feel new?

Date: _____

What problems are on your mind today? Do you have time to consider any of the main 10 issues? (List any practical, emotional, creative dilemmas/questions)

Did any encounter-book-movie-event change your perception of your dilemmas?

Did any solutions pop up in your mind? Where were you when it happened? What were you doing at the time?

Does anything feel new?

Make a list of new times - circumstances - places conducive to pop-up solutions

What is the most amazing thing you have discovered in the past two months?

*There is a need for fulfillment that is part of the   stuff of life itself, a need for personal adventure which is peculiar to man, a thirst for the absolute, which in the last analysis is an expression of a man's hunger and thirst after God. »*

Paul Tournier

# Re-evaluation

List up to 10 main problems/issues/struggles/worries on your mind now and compare them to your previous list 21 days ago.

Has anything changed?

If some problems went away what is life like without them?

What will be your next life adventure?

Notes

Printed in Great Britain
by Amazon

82380747R00064